W9-BSW-939

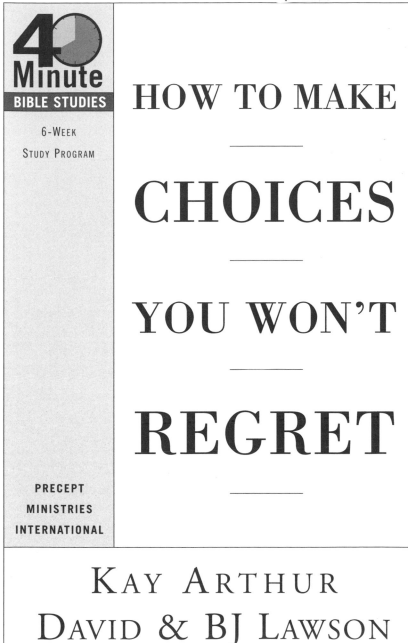

40 Minute
BIBLE STUDIES

6-WEEK

STUDY PROGRAM

HOW TO MAKE

CHOICES

YOU WON'T

REGRET

PRECEPT

MINISTRIES

INTERNATIONAL

KAY ARTHUR
DAVID & BJ LAWSON

HOW TO MAKE CHOICES YOU WON'T REGRET
PUBLISHED BY WATERBROOK PRESS
12265 Oracle Boulevard, Suite 200
Colorado Springs, Colorado 80921
A division of Random House, Inc.

All Scripture quotations, unless otherwise indicated, are taken from the *New American Standard Bible*® (NASB), © Copyright The Lockman Foundation 1960, 1962, 1963, 1968, 1971, 1972, 1973, 1975, 1977, 1995. Used by permission. (www.Lockman.org)

Italics in Scripture quotations reflect the author's added emphasis.

ISBN 978-1-57856-803-1

Copyright © 2003 by Precept Ministries International

Printed in the United States of America
2007

10 9 8

HOW TO USE THIS STUDY

This small-group study is for people who are interested in learning for themselves more about what the Bible says on various subjects, but who have only limited time to meet together. It's ideal, for example, for a lunch group at work, an early morning men's group, a young mother's group meeting in a home, a Sunday-school class, or even family devotions. (It's also ideal for small groups that typically have longer meeting times—such as evening groups or Saturday morning groups—but want to devote only a portion of their time together to actual study, while reserving the rest for prayer, fellowship, or other activities.)

This book is designed so that all the group's participants will complete each lesson's study activities *at the same time*. Discussing your insights drawn from what God says about the subject reveals exciting, life-impacting truths.

Although it's a group study, you'll need a facilitator to lead the study and keep the discussion moving. (This person's function is *not* that of a lecturer or teacher. However, when this book is used in a Sunday-school class or similar setting, the teacher should feel free to lead more directly and to bring in other insights in addition to those provided in each week's lesson.)

If *you* are your group's facilitator, the leader, here are some helpful points for making your job easier:

- Go through the lesson and mark the text before you lead the group. This will give you increased familiarity with the material and will enable you to facilitate the group with greater ease. It may be easier for you to lead the group through the instructions for marking if you as a leader choose a specific color for each symbol you mark.

- As you lead the group, start at the beginning of the text and simply read it aloud in the order it appears in the lesson, including the "insight boxes," which appear throughout. Work through the lesson together, observing and discussing what you learn. As you read the Scripture verses, have the group say aloud the word they are marking in the text.

- The discussion questions are there simply to help you cover the material. As the class moves into the discussion, many times you will find that they will cover the questions on their own. Remember, the discussion questions are there to guide the group through the topic, not to squelch discussion.

- Remember how important it is for people to verbalize their answers and discoveries. This greatly strengthens their personal understanding of each week's lesson. Try to ensure that everyone has plenty of opportunity to contribute to each week's discussions.

- Keep the discussion moving. This may mean spending more time on some parts of the study than on others. If necessary, you should feel free to spread out a lesson over more than one session. However, remember that you don't want to slow the pace too much. It's much better to leave everyone "wanting more" than to have people dropping out because of declining interest.

- If the validity or accuracy of some of the answers seems questionable, you can gently and cheerfully remind the group to stay focused on the truth of the Scriptures. Your object is to learn what the Bible says, not to engage in human philosophy. Simply stick with the Scriptures and give God the opportunity to speak. His Word *is* truth (John 17:17)!

HOW TO MAKE CHOICES YOU WON'T REGRET

I hate you! How can you stand there and say you love me? You don't call or come by except when you and your 'friend' don't have any plans or when I beg to see you! Don't tell me you love me!"

As his teenage daughter screamed, his heart was breaking. Finally he left, wondering, *How did I get to this point—divorced, with my daughter hating me? All I ever wanted was to be a great husband and father.*

Perhaps you, too, are wondering how you ended up where you are, whether your life would be better if you had made different decisions along the way. Maybe your current situation is great, but you're facing some difficult choices.

Every day we're faced with decisions, many of

which are benign, with no lasting consequences. Others have the potential to change the course of our lives—whether for good or bad. Certain avenues open to us are marked with hidden pitfalls or lead in harmful directions, and in some instances the wrong choice can even bring death. Where do you go for direction?

This inductive study will give you guidelines for making these difficult choices. By inductive we mean you will go straight to the source—the Bible—to see what God has to say. Knowing His Word for yourself will equip you to make choices that bring honor to Him and lead you to peace.

David was Israel's great and celebrated second king. His obedience had resulted in an unprecedented outpouring of blessing, not only on his household, but on all of Israel. A married man with a number of wives who had borne him many children, David had much about which to be thankful, but with his success came new opportunities and decisions. Let's take a look at this man David and the choices he made.

OBSERVE

Leader: Read aloud 2 Samuel 11:1-5.

• *Have the group say aloud and underline every reference to **David,** including pronouns.*

INSIGHT

It was normal for kings to go to war in the spring, which marks the end of the rainy season. The roads would be passable, there would be fodder for the animals, and an army on the move would be able to raid the fields for food.

DISCUSS

• What did you learn from marking *David* in verse 1?

2 SAMUEL 11:1-5

1 Then it happened in the spring, at the time when kings go out to battle, that David sent Joab and his servants with him and all Israel, and they destroyed the sons of Ammon and besieged Rabbah. But David stayed at Jerusalem.

2 Now when evening came, David arose from his bed and walked around on the roof of the king's house, and from the roof he saw a

woman bathing; and the woman was very beautiful in appearance.

³ So David sent and inquired about the woman. And one said, "Is this not Bathsheba, the daughter of Eliam, the wife of Uriah the Hittite?"

⁴ David sent messengers and took her, and when she came to him, he lay with her; and when she had purified herself from her uncleanness, she returned to her house.

⁵ The woman conceived; and she sent and told David, and said, "I am pregnant."

• What happened to David when he stayed home and didn't go to battle as kings should have?

INSIGHT

The woman David sees is "very beautiful." The Hebrew phrase used here is reserved for people of striking physical appearance.

• What course of events led to Bathsheba's pregnancy?

• What choices could David have made to change the outcome of this story?

OBSERVE

Did David have any information that would have helped him make the right choice? According to Deuteronomy 17:18-20, every king who came to power was supposed to write his own copy of the Law—the first five books of the Bible, Genesis through Deuteronomy. This means David would have written out Exodus 20:1-17, which lists the Ten Commandments.

Leader: Let's read these commandments.
- *Number each of the commandments as you read them. The first commandment is found in verse 3.*
- *When you come to a commandment that involves sexual activity, number it and put a check mark beside it: ✓*

DISCUSS

- Did David break any of these commandments when he slept with Bathsheba? If so, which ones?

EXODUS 20:1-17

1 Then God spoke all these words, saying,

2 "I am the LORD your God, who brought you out of the land of Egypt, out of the house of slavery.

3 "You shall have no other gods before Me.

4 "You shall not make for yourself an idol, or any likeness of what is in heaven above or on the earth beneath or in the water under the earth.

5 "You shall not worship them or serve them; for I, the LORD your God, am a jealous God, visiting the iniquity of the fathers on the children, on the third and the fourth

generations of those who hate Me,

⁶ but showing lovingkindness to thousands, to those who love Me and keep My commandments.

⁷ "You shall not take the name of the LORD your God in vain, for the LORD will not leave him unpunished who takes His name in vain.

⁸ "Remember the sabbath day, to keep it holy.

⁹ "Six days you shall labor and do all your work,

¹⁰ but the seventh day is a sabbath of the LORD your God; in it you shall not do any work, you or your son or your daughter, your

• Look back at what you marked about David in the passage from 2 Samuel. Was David made aware in any way that he would be breaking one or more of these commandments if he slept with Bathsheba?

• When David decided to sleep with Bathsheba, what was the basis of his choice?

• Do you see any similarities between what happened with David and Bathsheba and the choices many are making today? Explain your answer.

• When faced with a moral decision, what path are many people choosing and on what basis?

male or your female servant or your cattle or your sojourner who stays with you.

11 "For in six days the LORD made the heavens and the earth, the sea and all that is in them, and rested on the seventh day; therefore the LORD blessed the sabbath day and made it holy.

12 "Honor your father and your mother, that your days may be prolonged in the land which the LORD your God gives you.

13 "You shall not murder.

14 "You shall not commit adultery.

15 "You shall not steal.

16 "You shall not bear false witness against your neighbor.

17 "You shall not covet your neighbor's house; you shall not covet your neighbor's wife or his male servant or his female servant or his ox or his donkey or anything that belongs to your neighbor."

2 SAMUEL 11:6-13

6 Then David sent to Joab, saying, "Send me Uriah the Hittite." So Joab sent Uriah to David.

7 When Uriah came to him, David asked concerning the welfare of Joab and the people and the state of the war.

OBSERVE

Let's continue the story of David and Bathsheba.

Leader: Read aloud 2 Samuel 11:6-13.
  • *Have the group say aloud and underline every reference to* **David.**

INSIGHT

According to 1 Samuel 21:4-5, David and his men "kept themselves from women" whenever they set out to do battle.

DISCUSS

• What do you think David was trying to accomplish in verses 6-8, and why?

• Did his plan work? Why or why not?

• Was Uriah faced with any choices in this situation? What were they?

• What does Uriah's behavior tell you about his character?

8 Then David said to Uriah, "Go down to your house, and wash your feet." And Uriah went out of the king's house, and a present from the king was sent out after him.

9 But Uriah slept at the door of the king's house with all the servants of his lord, and did not go down to his house.

10 Now when they told David, saying, "Uriah did not go down to his house," David said to Uriah, "Have you not come from a journey? Why did you not go down to your house?"

11 Uriah said to David, "The ark and Israel and Judah are staying in temporary shelters, and my lord Joab and the servants of my lord are camping in the open field. Shall I then go to my house to eat and to drink and to lie with my wife? By your life and the life of your soul, I will not do this thing."

12 Then David said to Uriah, "Stay here today also, and tomorrow I will let you go." So Uriah remained in Jerusalem that day and the next.

13 Now David called him, and he ate and drank before him, and he made him drunk; and in the evening he went out to lie on his bed with his lord's servants, but he did not go down to his house.

• How do you suppose David felt in this situation and why?

• What did David choose to do when Uriah wouldn't go home? Why?

• Have you ever seen or heard of a scheme like David's in verse 13? Describe what happened.

OBSERVE

Leader: *Read 2 Samuel 11:14-17 aloud.*
Have the group do the following:

- *Underline every reference to **David**.*
- *Draw a box around every reference to* ***Uriah:*** ☐

DISCUSS

- What was David's next strategy in regard to Uriah?

- Who was he involving?

- Why was David going to all this trouble?

- What was the end result of this strategic move, and how did it measure up to the Ten Commandments? What had David just done?

2 SAMUEL 11:14-17

14 Now in the morning David wrote a letter to Joab and sent it by the hand of Uriah.

15 He had written in the letter, saying, "Place Uriah in the front line of the fiercest battle and withdraw from him, so that he may be struck down and die."

16 So it was as Joab kept watch on the city, that he put Uriah at the place where he knew there were valiant men.

17 The men of the city went out and fought against Joab, and some of the people among David's servants fell; and Uriah the Hittite also died.

2 SAMUEL 11:26-27

26 Now when the wife of Uriah heard that Uriah her husband was dead, she mourned for her husband.

27 When the time of mourning was over, David sent and brought her to his house and she became his wife; then she bore him a son. But the thing that David had done was evil in the sight of the LORD.

OBSERVE

Leader: Read aloud 2 Samuel 11:26-27. Have the group do the following:
  • *Underline the references to* **David.**
  • *Circle every reference to* **Bathsheba.**

DISCUSS

• What did you learn from marking the references to Bathsheba?

• What did God think about all that David had done?

• Discuss one by one the things David did that God considers evil.

• Review the choices David made at each juncture, beginning with not going to war when it was time for kings to do so, right through to the last scripture you read. As you discuss this, talk about the choices he should have made.

• What have you learned from the events in this chapter that you can apply to your life today?

WRAP IT UP

God refers to David as "a man after His own heart" (1 Samuel 13:14; Acts 13:22). This description is reflected in David's earlier choices to follow God's commands and statutes, choices that resulted in blessings not only for him but for the entire nation of Israel. But in his life we also see a series of choices to go against God's commands, commands with which he was intimately familiar.

David could have chosen to obey God's Word at any point in time, but instead he chose to continue on a path that took him further and further into danger. A seemingly insignificant choice to stay home from battle led to his coveting a neighbor's wife, which in turn led to adultery and murder. David's actions were evil in the sight of the Lord.

What about you? Are you known as a man or woman after God's heart, or have you done evil in the sight of the Lord? Are you making choices based on the Word of God or on your own desires? If the latter is the case, know this: You can choose to follow the Word of God at any time and turn from the path that leads to disaster.

David's third cover-up appears to have succeeded. He has taken Bathsheba for his wife, and she has borne him a son. David's bad choices are his own little secret. No one will find out…or will they?

OBSERVE

Leader: *Read 2 Samuel 12:1-6 aloud.*

   • *Have the group underline the references to **David**.*

DISCUSS

• What did you learn from marking *David*?

2 SAMUEL 12:1-6

1 Then the LORD sent Nathan to David. And he came to him, and said, "There were two men in one city, the one rich and the other poor.

2 "The rich man had a great many flocks and herds.

3 "But the poor man had nothing except one little ewe lamb which he bought and nourished; and it grew up together with him and his children. It would eat of his bread and drink of his cup and lie in his bosom, and was like a daughter to him.

4 "Now a traveler came to the rich man, and he was unwilling to take from his own flock or his own herd, to prepare for the wayfarer who had come to him; rather he took the poor man's ewe lamb and prepared it for the man who had come to him."

5 Then David's anger burned greatly against the man, and he said to Nathan, "As the LORD lives, surely the man who has done this deserves to die.

6 "He must make restitution for the lamb fourfold, because he did this thing and had no compassion."

• What was happening in these six verses?

• Why was Nathan telling this parable to David?

OBSERVE

Leader: Read 2 Samuel 12:7-9 aloud. Have your group say aloud and mark…

- *every reference to **God**, including pronouns and synonyms, with a triangle:* △
- *every mention of **David** by underlining it.*

DISCUSS

- What did you learn about God from marking the references to Him?

- What did you learn about David?

- What are the parallels between the parable Nathan just told David and the king's own situation? Discuss them.

- What was Nathan's role in all this? What made it difficult, and why?

- What choice did Nathan have to make?

- Have you ever been in a situation similar to Nathan's? Describe the situation and

2 SAMUEL 12:7-9

7 Nathan then said to David, "You are the man! Thus says the LORD God of Israel, 'It is I who anointed you king over Israel and it is I who delivered you from the hand of Saul.

8 'I also gave you your master's house and your master's wives into your care, and I gave you the house of Israel and Judah; and if that had been too little, I would have added to you many more things like these!

9 'Why have you despised the word of the LORD by doing evil in His sight? You have struck down Uriah the Hittite with the sword, have taken

his wife to be your wife, and have killed him with the sword of the sons of Ammon.

how you handled it. What was the outcome?

• What did Nathan mean when he said David despised the Word of the Lord? How did this affect David's choices?

• Do you know someone who despised the Word of the Lord? If you can, describe the situation as well as the consequences, but keep the person anonymous.

2 SAMUEL 12:10-14

10 'Now therefore, the sword shall never depart from your house, because you have despised Me and have taken the wife of Uriah the Hittite to be your wife.'

11 "Thus says the LORD, 'Behold, I will raise up evil against you from your own household; I will even take

OBSERVE

Leader: *Read 2 Samuel 12:10-14 aloud. Notice that Nathan continues to speak for God.*

> • *Underline every reference to **David.***
> • *Draw a triangle over every reference to the **Lord,** including pronouns.*

DISCUSS

• What were the consequences of David's choice to despise the Word of the Lord?

• Were others affected by David's sin? If so, list who was affected and describe how.

• How did David respond to Nathan's message from God and what can you learn from it?

• What have you learned about God from marking these verses?

• How could knowing what happens in this chapter affect your life and your choices?

your wives before your eyes and give them to your companion, and he will lie with your wives in broad daylight.

12 'Indeed you did it secretly, but I will do this thing before all Israel, and under the sun.' "

13 Then David said to Nathan, "I have sinned against the LORD." And Nathan said to David, "The LORD also has taken away your sin; you shall not die.

14 "However, because by this deed you have given occasion to the enemies of the LORD to blaspheme, the child also that is born to you shall surely die."

WRAP IT UP

Last week we saw how important it is that the choices we make be governed by our knowledge of God's Word. We've observed David's temptation and his response, a response that shows he "despised the word of the Lord" (2 Samuel 12:9). He chose to disobey three of God's commandments: "You shall not covet your neighbor's wife," "You shall not commit adultery," and "You shall not murder."

These sins were committed in secret—or so David thought. God knew, however, and He chose to reveal the truth to Israel and to the world.

Have you made wrong choices that you think no one knows about? Perhaps you're involved in pornography, coveting your neighbor's wife or husband, an affair?

When confronted by the prophet Nathan, David chose repentance, returning to God. David was not simply sorry he got caught. He recognized his sin as an offense against a holy God, and he turned from it. God in His mercy spared him from the death he deserved. However, confession and repentance could not take away the severe consequences of David's sin, which affected not only him, but also his family and, ultimately, a whole nation.

Your sin, like David's, has the potential to destroy you, your family, and your community. The choice is yours. Know God, follow His commandments, and receive blessing upon blessing. Or choose to follow after your own desires and suffer the consequences—consequences of God's choosing, consequences that can last a lifetime.

What if you have made some wrong choices in your life? Does that mean it's too late to change? Will you be thrown in the corner, wadded up, made useless to God or man?

Have you ever done something and wished you could do it over, have a fresh start? Is there a way to wipe your slate clean and begin again?

King David went down in the annals of history as a man after God's own heart. Yet we know from our earlier studies that he made some poor choices, choices that affected him and many around him, choices that led to the death of one of his mighty men and his own son. How can we reconcile David's disobedience with God's opinion of him?

This week let's take a look at David's repentance and God's grace and loving-kindness.

OBSERVE

The introduction to Psalm 51 tells us when it was written: "For the choir director. A Psalm of David, when Nathan the prophet came to him, after he had gone in to Bathsheba."

Leader: Read Psalm 51:1-4 aloud. Have the group do the following:
- *Underline every pronoun referring to **David.***
- *Put an **S** over every reference to **sin**, including **transgression, iniquity,** and **doing evil.***

PSALM 51:1-4

¹ Be gracious to me, O God, according to Your lovingkindness; according to the greatness of Your compassion blot out my transgressions.

² Wash me thoroughly from my iniquity and cleanse me from my sin.

³ For I know my transgressions, and my sin is ever before me.

⁴ Against You, You only, I have sinned and done what is evil in Your sight, so that You are justified when You speak and blameless when You judge.

DISCUSS

• What did you learn from marking the references to David?

OBSERVE

Leader: *Read Psalm 51:1-4 again. This time have the group say aloud the following words and mark them:*

* *Put a triangle over every reference to* **God,** *including pronouns.*
* *Put a box around each* **according to.**

DISCUSS

• What did you learn from marking the references to God?

• What was David making a choice to do? Look at the phrase *according to,* which you marked, and discuss the basis of David's request for God's grace and cleansing.

INSIGHT

In David's search for forgiveness of his sins, he opens his heart. In this passage he uses three words for sin to express the seriousness of his behavior: *transgressions*, which means "rebellion;" *iniquity*, which means "crooked dealings;" and *sin*, which indicates error and wandering. In the New Testament, *sin* means "to miss the mark," to fail to live up to the standard.

OBSERVE

Leader: Read Psalm 51:5-12 aloud. Have the group call out the following key words as they mark them:

- *Underline every pronoun referring to **David**.*
- *Mark **sin** with its synonyms, as you did previously.*

PSALM 51:5-12

5 Behold, I was brought forth in iniquity, and in sin my mother conceived me.

6 Behold, You desire truth in the innermost being, and in the hidden part You will make me know wisdom.

7 Purify me with hyssop, and I shall be clean; wash me, and I shall be whiter than snow.

8 Make me to hear joy and gladness, let the bones which You have broken rejoice.

9 Hide Your face from my sins and blot out all my iniquities.

10 Create in me a clean heart, O God, and renew a steadfast spirit within me.

11 Do not cast me away from Your presence and do not take Your Holy Spirit from me.

12 Restore to me the joy of Your salvation and sustain me with a willing spirit.

DISCUSS

• What did you learn from marking the references to David?

OBSERVE

Leader: *Read through Psalm 51:5-12 again.*

• *This time mark every reference to* **God** *with a triangle, as before.*

DISCUSS

• What did you learn about God from marking the references to Him?

• Have you discovered anything new about God through this psalm? How might this affect your attitude or relationship with Him?

• In dealing with your own sin, do you see the seriousness of what you have done? Do you realize that your actions are against a holy and just God? How does knowing this affect the choices you make in regard to your sin?

• What were the benefits David sought—and that anyone, including you, can receive—when he chose to confess his sin and seek God's forgiveness?

INSIGHT

David prayed that the Lord, like a priest, would cleanse him from his sin. In Leviticus 14:1-7 the unclean, such as lepers, were instructed to present themselves before the priest on the occasion of their purification. The priest, being satisfied that the unclean person had met the requirements for purification, would dip a bunch of hyssop (a fragrant herb) in water, then sprinkle the person, symbolic of ritual cleansing.

PSALM 51:13-17

13 Then I will teach transgressors Your ways, and sinners will be converted to You.

14 Deliver me from bloodguiltiness, O God, the God of my salvation; then my tongue will joyfully sing of Your righteousness.

15 O Lord, open my lips, that my mouth may declare Your praise.

16 For You do not delight in sacrifice, otherwise I would give it; You are not pleased with burnt offering.

17 The sacrifices of God are a broken spirit; a broken and a contrite heart, O God, You will not despise.

OBSERVE

Leader: Read Psalm 51:13-17. Have the group say aloud and mark every reference to:
- **God,** including **You** and **Your,** with a triangle, as before.
- **David,** with an underline.

DISCUSS

- In verses 13-17, what did David say he would do as a result of God's forgiveness and restoration?

- What did you learn from marking God?

- According to verse 17, what is the prerequisite for spiritual renewal?

- What do you think God means by "a broken spirit" and "a broken and contrite heart"? What would this look like in a person's life?

- So often today we hear people saying, "I know God's forgiven me, but I cannot forgive myself." Did David talk at all about forgiving himself?

• Nowhere does the Bible speak about people forgiving themselves. According to this psalm, why is this unnecessary? What would choices have to do with this situation?

• Have you ever had the opportunity, after receiving forgiveness and restoration for wrong choices, to use your experience to instruct others about God's ways? Take a few minutes to share this with the group.

OBSERVE

Leader: Read the last two verses of Psalm 51 aloud.

• *Have the group say and mark every reference to* **God***, including* **You** *and* **Your***.*

DISCUSS

• What was David's closing request in these verses?

PSALM 51:18-19

18 By Your favor do good to Zion; build the walls of Jerusalem.

19 Then You will delight in righteous sacrifices, in burnt offering and whole burnt offering; then young bulls will be offered on Your altar.

• Last week we saw that an individual's sin can have far-reaching consequences. It can impact our families, churches, communities, and nation. Because of his sin, David was concerned for the welfare of his nation. In what ways do our individual choices—in the area of morals—impact our nation as a whole?

OBSERVE

Before we bring this week's study to a close, let's take a look at another scripture that will help us see how God's mercy and grace are extended toward us when we make wrong choices.

1 JOHN 1:9

If we confess our sins, He is faithful and righteous to forgive us our sins and to cleanse us from all unrighteousness.

Leader: Read 1 John 1:9 aloud. Have the group call out the following key words as they mark them:

- *Mark every reference to **God** or **He** as before.*
- *Underline every reference to **we** or **us**.*

INSIGHT

The Greek word for *confess* means "to say the same thing as," therefore "to agree with" God that what you have done is wrong. The word for *forgiveness* carries the idea of "a cancellation of debts" or "a dismissal of charges." It means "to send away."

DISCUSS

• What is our responsibility in this verse?

• According to this verse, what is God's response to our confession?

• On what basis are we forgiven?

• If you have made some wrong choices, what reassurance can you find in this verse? Can God ever use you again? Why?

WRAP IT UP

God sent the prophet Nathan to confront David with his sin. Nathan's rebuke cut to the very core of David's soul, leaving him deeply, painfully aware of sin, of having offended God, of his desperate need for God's grace. In Psalm 51, we see that David threw himself on God's mercy; he had no other choice.

Maybe you, like David, have made some wrong choices. Has the Holy Spirit brought conviction of sin to you? If so, have you seen the seriousness of it? Do you realize your sin is against a holy and just God? If so, what do you do?

1. Confess your sin. In other words, agree with God that what you have done is wrong.

2. Take responsibility for that sin. You cannot blame anyone else. You made the choice to do what you did.

3. Thank God for the blood of Jesus Christ, which cleanses you from all sin, and accept in faith His forgiveness. (Forgiveness is always on the basis of grace, never merit. Remember that God's forgiveness is based on His love and compassion, not on our worthiness.)

4. Take God at His Word. No matter how you feel, cling in faith to what God says. Don't allow the accuser, Satan, to rob you of your victory.

Having done these things, out of a heart of gratitude for all God has done for you, use this as an opportunity to instruct and minister to those around you who have also made wrong choices.

King Josiah, Judah's sixteenth king, was the godliest of all the kings in Israel from the time of David. He began well, continued well, and ended well. He was also the last king of Judah who "did right in the sight of the LORD." Let's take a look at his life and the choices he made that won him such a reputation.

OBSERVE

Leader: Read 2 Kings 22:1-2.
- *Underline very reference to **Josiah**, including the pronouns.*
- *Draw a cloud shape like this* around *any reference to **doing what is right in the sight of the Lord.***

DISCUSS

- What did you learn from marking *Josiah*? Who was he, where did he live, what did he do, and what was he like as a person?

- You saw that David, the king we just studied, is referred to as Josiah's father. If Josiah walked like David, as this verse indicates, did he walk in a right way or a wrong way? Explain how you know?

2 KINGS 22:1-2

1 Josiah was eight years old when he became king, and he reigned thirty-one years in Jerusalem; and his mother's name was Jedidah the daughter of Adaiah of Bozkath.

2 And he did right in the sight of the LORD and walked in all the way of his father David, nor did he turn aside to the right or to the left.

2 KINGS 21:10-16

10 Now the LORD spoke through His servants the prophets, saying,

11 "Because Manasseh king of Judah has done these abominations, having done wickedly more than all the Amorites did who were before him, and has also made Judah sin with his idols;

12 therefore thus says the LORD, the God of Israel, 'Behold, I am bringing such calamity on Jerusalem and Judah, that whoever hears of it, both his ears shall tingle.

13 'I will stretch over Jerusalem the line of Samaria and the plummet of the house of Ahab, and I will wipe

OBSERVE

Josiah was listed in the genealogy of King David; however, his biological father was Amon, the son of Manasseh. Like Josiah, both Amon and Manasseh were kings of Judah in the southern kingdom.

Leader: *Read 2 Kings 21:10-16 aloud. Have the group do the following:*
- *Underline every reference to **Manasseh**.*
- *Draw a box around every reference to **doing evil in the sight of the Lord**.*

DISCUSS

• Let's look at the familial heritage of Josiah. What did you learn in this passage about Manasseh, the grandfather of King Josiah?

Jerusalem as one wipes a dish, wiping it and turning it upside down.

14 'I will abandon the remnant of My inheritance and deliver them into the hand of their enemies, and they shall become as plunder and spoil to all their enemies;

15 because they have done evil in My sight, and have been provoking Me to anger since the day their fathers came from Egypt, even to this day.' "

16 Moreover, Manasseh shed very much innocent blood until he had filled Jerusalem from one end to another; besides his sin with which he made Judah sin, in doing evil in the sight of the LORD.

2 KINGS 21:18-24

¹⁸ And Manasseh slept with his fathers and was buried in the garden of his own house, in the garden of Uzza, and Amon his son became king in his place.

¹⁹ Amon was twenty-two years old when he became king, and he reigned two years in Jerusalem; and his mother's name was Meshullemeth the daughter of Haruz of Jotbah.

²⁰ He did evil in the sight of the LORD, as Manasseh his father had done.

²¹ For he walked in all the way that his father had walked, and

OBSERVE

Leader: Read 2 Kings 21:18-24. Have the group...
- *underline every reference to **Amon**, the father of Josiah.*
- *draw a box around every reference to **doing evil in the sight of the Lord.***

DISCUSS

- What did you learn about Amon from the text?

• Thinking back to the two verses you read about Josiah in 2 Kings 22, do you see differences among Josiah and Amon and Manasseh?

• What does this tell you about a person's heritage? Do we have to be like our fathers and mothers, our grandfathers and grandmothers? Do we have a choice to be different? Explain your answer.

served the idols that his father had served and worshiped them.

22 So he forsook the LORD, the God of his fathers, and did not walk in the way of the LORD.

23 The servants of Amon conspired against him and killed the king in his own house.

24 Then the people of the land killed all those who had conspired against King Amon, and the people of the land made Josiah his son king in his place.

2 CHRONICLES 34:1-8

¹ Josiah was eight years old when he became king, and he reigned thirty-one years in Jerusalem.

² And he did right in the sight of the LORD, and walked in the ways of his father David and did not turn aside to the right or to the left.

³ For in the eighth year of his reign while he was still a youth, he began to seek the God of his father David; and in the twelfth year he began to purge Judah and Jerusalem of the high places, the Asherim, the carved images, and the molten images.

OBSERVE

Something momentous happened in the eighteenth year of King Josiah's reign, as we shall read about later in 2 Kings 22. But before we go there, we need to learn about his early years as king and the choices that shaped his reign.

Leader: Read 2 Chronicles 34:1-8 aloud. Have the group...

• *underline every reference to Josiah.*

• *draw a cloud around every reference to doing right in the sight of the Lord.*

DISCUSS

• How old was Josiah in verse 3 and what did he choose to do at this time in his life?

• What did you learn from marking *Josiah*?

• In light of the time in which Josiah lived, were his choices in keeping with the society, the culture around him? How do you know?

• How does this relate to the time we are living in today and the choices we make?

4 They tore down the altars of the Baals in his presence, and the incense altars that were high above them he chopped down; also the Asherim, the carved images and the molten images he broke in pieces and ground to powder and scattered it on the graves of those who had sacrificed to them.

5 Then he burned the bones of the priests on their altars and purged Judah and Jerusalem.

6 In the cities of Manasseh, Ephraim, Simeon, even as far as Naphtali, in their surrounding ruins,

7 he also tore down the altars and beat the Asherim and the carved images into powder, and chopped down all the incense altars throughout the land of Israel. Then he returned to Jerusalem.

8 Now in the eighteenth year of his reign, when he had purged the land and the house, he sent Shaphan the son of Azaliah, and Maaseiah an official of the city, and Joah the son of Joahaz the recorder, to repair the house of the LORD his God.

• What did Josiah decide to do in the eighteenth year of his reign?

• How old was he at this time? For how many years had he been actively serving the Lord?

• What application can you find in Josiah's story for your life today? If you work with youth, what are you doing to prepare them to serve the Lord as Josiah did? If you are a youth, what are you doing to serve the Lord?

OBSERVE

Now let's return to 2 Kings 22 to see the impact of Josiah's choices. The time was approximately 622 B.C., the eighteenth year of Josiah's reign. He was twenty-six years old.

Leader: Read 2 Kings 22:3-13 aloud and have the group do the following:

- *Draw a cloud around every reference to* **the house of the Lord.**
- *Draw a box around every reference to* **the book of the Law or the book.**

INSIGHT

The phrase "house of the Lord" refers to the permanent temple built by Solomon, the place where the children of Israel were to worship God. They were not to worship at any other altars.

DISCUSS

- What did you learn from this passage about the house of the Lord and about Israel's attitude toward it?

2 KINGS 22:3-13

3 Now in the eighteenth year of King Josiah, the king sent Shaphan, the son of Azaliah the son of Meshullam the scribe, to the house of the LORD saying,

4 "Go up to Hilkiah the high priest that he may count the money brought in to the house of the LORD which the doorkeepers have gathered from the people.

5 "Let them deliver it into the hand of the workmen who have the oversight of the house of the LORD, and let them give it to the workmen who are in the house of the LORD to repair the damages of the house,

6 to the carpenters and the builders and the masons and for buying timber and hewn stone to repair the house.

7 "Only no accounting shall be made with them for the money delivered into their hands, for they deal faithfully."

8 Then Hilkiah the high priest said to Shaphan the scribe, "I have found the book of the law in the house of the LORD." And Hilkiah gave the book to Shaphan who read it.

9 Shaphan the scribe came to the king and brought back word to the king and said, "Your servants have

• What did you learn from marking the references to the book of the Law?

• Do you see any parallels in our churches today in respect to the book of the Law being lost in the house of the Lord? Explain your answer.

• How did Josiah respond when he heard the words from the book of the Law? Be specific in the details of his response.

• According to verse 13, what was the problem and why?

emptied out the money that was found in the house, and have delivered it into the hand of the workmen who have the oversight of the house of the LORD."

10 Moreover, Shaphan the scribe told the king saying, "Hilkiah the priest has given me a book." And Shaphan read it in the presence of the king.

• How do you respond when you hear the words of the Bible?

11 When the king heard the words of the book of the law, he tore his clothes.

12 Then the king commanded Hilkiah the priest, Ahikam the son of Shaphan, Achbor the son of Micaiah, Shaphan the scribe, and Asaiah the king's servant saying,

13 "Go, inquire of the LORD for me and the people and all Judah concerning the words of this book that has been found, for great is the wrath of the LORD that burns against us, because our fathers have not listened to the words of this book, to do according to all that is written concerning us."

• What choices was Josiah making at this point? Why was he making them?

---

2 KINGS 22:14-20

14 So Hilkiah the priest, Ahikam, Achbor, Shaphan, and Asaiah went to Huldah the prophetess, the wife of Shallum the son of Tikvah, the son of Harhas, keeper of the wardrobe (now she lived in Jerusalem in the Second

OBSERVE

Leader: Read 2 Kings 22:14-20. Have the group do the following:

• *Mark every reference to the **Lord** with a triangle:* △

• *Draw a box around every reference to **the book:*** ☐

• *Mark every occurrence of **listened** or **heard** with a symbol like an ear:* ◝

DISCUSS

• What did you learn from marking the references to the Lord?

OBSERVE

Leader: *Read 2 Kings 22:14-20 again.*

• *This time have the group underline every reference to* **Josiah.**

DISCUSS

• What promise did the Lord make to Josiah, as told by the prophetess Huldah? Why did He make this promise? Be specific in your answer.

Quarter); and they spoke to her.

15 She said to them, "Thus says the LORD God of Israel, 'Tell the man who sent you to me,

16 thus says the LORD, "Behold, I bring evil on this place and on its inhabitants, even all the words of the book which the king of Judah has read.

17 "Because they have forsaken Me and have burned incense to other gods that they might provoke Me to anger with all the work of their hands, therefore My wrath burns against this place, and it shall not be quenched." '

18 "But to the king of Judah who sent you to inquire of the LORD thus shall you say to him, 'Thus says the LORD God of Israel, "Regarding the words which you have heard,

19 because your heart was tender and you humbled yourself before the LORD when you heard what I spoke against this place and against its inhabitants that they should become a desolation and a curse, and you have torn your clothes and wept before Me, I truly have heard you," declares the LORD.

20 "Therefore, behold, I will gather you to your fathers, and you

• What did you learn from marking the references to the book? How would you describe the importance of choosing to listen to it?

• What do you think will happen to our families, our churches, our nation if we choose to disregard the Word of God, the Bible?

OBSERVE

Leader: *Read 2 Kings 23:1-3. Have the group do the following:*

• *Underline every reference to **Josiah**.*

• *Mark every reference to **the book**.*

• *Put a **C** over every occurrence of the word **covenant**.*

INSIGHT

A covenant is a solemn, binding agreement between two parties—one lesser and one greater, or both of equal status—who commit themselves to each other under certain conditions. A covenant is never to be broken.

---

will be gathered to your grave in peace, and your eyes will not see all the evil which I will bring on this place.'"'"

So they brought back word to the king.

2 KINGS 23:1-3

¹ Then the king sent, and they gathered to him all the elders of Judah and of Jerusalem.

² The king went up to the house of the LORD and all the men of Judah and all the inhabitants of Jerusalem with him, and the priests and the prophets and all the people, both small and great; and he read in their hearing all the words of the book of

the covenant which was found in the house of the LORD.

3 And the king stood by the pillar and made a covenant before the LORD, to walk after the LORD, and to keep His commandments and His testimonies and His statutes with all his heart and all his soul, to carry out the words of this covenant that were written in this book. And all the people entered into the covenant.

DISCUSS

• What did you learn from marking the references to King Josiah? Where did he go and what did he do?

• What commitments were made as part of the covenant?

• What did the people choose to do?

• Now what choices have you made in respect to the Word of God? Have you fully considered the ramifications of your choice?

WRAP IT UP

Manasseh, Josiah's grandfather, was the worst of all the kings of Judah. He did evil in the sight of the Lord and built altars to foreign gods in the house of the Lord. Amon, Josiah's father, also forsook the Lord and followed in the sinful path of his own father.

When Josiah was confronted with the truth of the Word of God at an early age, he had a choice to make. He could either continue to walk in the way of his father and grandfather, not listening to the words of the book, or he could break the cycle of sin. He could heed and obey all that was written in the book.

Josiah's choice? He humbled himself before the Lord and took action, with a heart made tender by God's Word. As a result, he had the privilege of leading his people in a great revival.

What about you? Is your heart tender? Are you willing to humble yourself before the Lord and break the cycle of sin in your family, church, community, and nation? Maybe you think you are too young— or perhaps too old. But we have seen that God will honor a tender heart no matter what the age.

Will you make a covenant before the Lord to walk after Him and keep His commandments? Are you willing to "tear down" (expose) the high places and urge others to turn from false gods and back toward the one true God? What if choosing this path means going against the culture of your day? Standing firm against your peers and relatives for the sake of what is right, pure, and good? Are you willing to be the vessel the Lord uses to bring a great revival in this day?

How do you respond when faced with temptation? How do you decide what to do? One way we can learn to make wise choices is by observing the examples of those who have gone before us. Let's look at the first choice ever made by a human being faced with temptation. Then we'll observe how Jesus faced temptation. On what did He base His responses and how did they differ from those of Adam and Eve?

OBSERVE

To examine the first choice made by a human being in response to temptation, we must go to Genesis chapter 2.

Leader: *Read Genesis 2:15-17. Have the group do the following:*
  • *Underline every reference to* **man.**
  • *Put a tombstone shaped figure over the word* **die,** *like this:* ⋂

DISCUSS

• The man to whom God was speaking was Adam, the man He created from the dust of the earth. What did you learn from marking the references to the man?

GENESIS 2:15-17

15 Then the LORD God took the man and put him into the garden of Eden to cultivate it and keep it.

16 The LORD God commanded the man, saying, "From any tree of the garden you may eat freely;

17 but from the tree of the knowledge of good and evil you shall not eat, for in the day that you eat from it you will surely die."

• Man and God lived in perfect oneness. One thing—and only one thing—was forbidden to the man. What was it?

• Was man given a choice in respect to his relationship with God? What was it?

• Were any consequences tied to his choice? Was this made plain? Explain your answer.

GENESIS 3:1-6

¹ Now the serpent was more crafty than any beast of the field which the LORD God had made. And he said to the woman, "Indeed, has God said, 'You shall not eat from any tree of the garden'?"

² The woman said to the serpent, "From the fruit of the trees of the garden we may eat;

OBSERVE

As we've seen, God placed Adam—and Eve, his wife—in a garden, referred to as the Garden of Eden in Genesis 3:23. They lived in freedom with only one restriction. Sounds simple enough, doesn't it? Let's see how they responded.

Leader: Read Genesis 3:1-6. Have the group do the following:

- *Underline every reference to the **woman**.*
- *Draw a pitchfork over every reference to the **serpent**, like this:* ⨉
- *Put a tombstone over every reference to **dying**, as before:* ⬠

DISCUSS

• What did you learn from marking the references to the serpent?

• What did you learn from marking the references to the woman?

• What was the woman faced with in these verses?

• Did she know the consequences of her choice?

• How did she respond?

• Circle all the verbs in verse 6 that relate directly to the woman. Do you see any similarity between the actions that led her to sin and the actions that led King David to sin? (See lesson 1.) If so, describe them.

3 but from the fruit of the tree which is in the middle of the garden, God has said, 'You shall not eat from it or touch it, or you will die.' "

4 The serpent said to the woman, "You surely will not die!

5 "For God knows that in the day you eat from it your eyes will be opened, and you will be like God, knowing good and evil."

6 When the woman saw that the tree was good for food, and that it was a delight to the eyes, and that the tree was desirable to make one wise, she took from its fruit and ate; and she gave also to her husband with her, and he ate.

LUKE 4:1-13

1 Jesus, full of the Holy Spirit, returned from the Jordan and was led around by the Spirit in the wilderness

2 for forty days, being tempted by the devil. And He ate nothing during those days, and when they had ended, He became hungry.

3 And the devil said to Him, "If You are the Son of God, tell this stone to become bread."

4 And Jesus answered him, "It is written, 'Man shall not live on bread alone.'"

5 And he led Him up and showed Him all the kingdoms of the world in a moment of time.

OBSERVE

Leader: Read aloud Luke 4:1-13. Have the group do the following:

• Mark every reference to **Jesus**, including pronouns, with a cross: †

• Put a pitchfork over every reference to **the devil**:

• Draw a box around the phrases "**it is written**" and "**it is said**":

DISCUSS

• What did you learn from marking Jesus in this passage?

• What did you learn from marking the devil?

• What was the devil doing to Jesus? Had he done this to anyone before? Who was the first one?

OBSERVE

Leader: Read through the passage aloud once more. This time...

- *Have the group number the temptations the devil set forth. Then discuss each temptation, being sure to talk about Jesus' response each time.*

DISCUSS

- How did the devil change his tactic with the third temptation? And why?

- How did Jesus respond to this?

- According to verse 13, had the devil given up on tempting Jesus? When would He be tempted again?

6 And the devil said to Him, "I will give You all this domain and its glory; for it has been handed over to me, and I give it to whomever I wish.

7 "Therefore if You worship before me, it shall all be Yours."

8 Jesus answered him, "It is written, 'You shall worship the LORD your God and serve Him only.'"

9 And he led Him to Jerusalem and had Him stand on the pinnacle of the temple, and said to Him, "If You are the Son of God, throw Yourself down from here;

10 for it is written, 'He will command His angels concerning You to guard You,'

11 and, 'On their hands they will bear You up, so that You will not strike Your foot against a stone.' "

12 And Jesus answered and said to him, "It is said, 'You shall not put the LORD your God to the test.' "

13 When the devil had finished every temptation, he left Him until an opportune time.

• What did you learn from comparing the way Eve responded to the devil's temptation with how Jesus handled it? Why did one succeed and the other fail? Remember, the Bible says Jesus was a man tempted in all the ways we are.

• Is there anything you learned personally from these last two passages about dealing with temptation and making choices? If so, describe how this will guide you in the future.

OBSERVE

Jesus obviously considered the Word to be an important part of His decision-making process. Let's take a look at what Paul had to say about the Word of God.

Leader: Read aloud 2 Timothy 3:16-17. Have the group do the following:

- *Mark each reference to **God** with a triangle:* △
- *Put a box around **Scripture**:* ▭

INSIGHT

Inspired literally means "God breathed." All Scripture is breathed by God and is profitable, which means "useful, beneficial, or to your advantage."

2 TIMOTHY 3:16-17

16 All Scripture is inspired by God and profitable for teaching, for reproof, for correction, for training in righteousness;

17 so that the man of God may be adequate, equipped for every good work.

DISCUSS

- Where does Scripture come from and what is its purpose?

- According to this passage, how much of Scripture is inspired?

INSIGHT

Teaching means "giving instruction." It includes the act of teaching and imparting knowledge. *Reproof* means "conviction," revealing where one is wrong. *Correction* means "to set straight." In other words, Scripture instructs us, imparts truth to us, and shows us where we are wrong—but doesn't leave us there. Scripture sets us straight and then continues to train us in righteousness, which means that the Word of God enables us to know what is right and wrong and how to live in a way that pleases God.

• Number each of the benefits of Scripture listed in this passage, in other words, the uses for which it is "profitable." Then discuss how each of these benefits would help you in the decision-making process.

• If you know the Word of God and allow it to work in you, then what, according to verse 17, will be the end result?

OBSERVE

As we have seen in studying 2 Timothy 3:16-17, the Word of God serves a clear purpose in guiding us to wise choices. It should be a treasured resource for every person who desires to follow God, yet how many of us neglect to study it, to meditate on its truths?

Let's take a look at Psalm 119 to learn what our attitude should be toward the Word of God.

Leader: Read aloud Psalm 119:97-104. Have the group say aloud the following words and mark them as indicated:

- *Underline every* ***I, me,*** *and* ***my,*** *pronouns that refer to the* ***psalmist.***
- *Put a triangle over every reference to* ***God,*** *including* ***You*** *and* ***Your.***

DISCUSS

- Beginning with verse 97, read through the Psalm again and record what you learned from marking every reference to the psalmist.

PSALM 119:97-104

97 O how I love Your law! It is my meditation all the day.

98 Your commandments make me wiser than my enemies, for they are ever mine.

99 I have more insight than all my teachers, for Your testimonies are my meditation.

100 I understand more than the aged, because I have observed Your precepts.

101 I have restrained my feet from every evil way, that I may keep Your word.

102 I have not turned aside from Your ordinances, for You Yourself have taught me.

103 How sweet are Your words to my taste! Yes, sweeter than honey to my mouth!

104 From Your precepts I get understanding; therefore I hate every false way.

• According to what we have seen in this psalm, how would knowing the Word affect the choices you make?

• Is it possible to make choices that keep you from following a wrong and disastrous path? Explain your answer.

WRAP IT UP

This week we saw that Eve, when faced with temptation by the serpent, made her choice based on the desire of her flesh rather than on the Word of God. The serpent presented her the truth with "a twist of lie." She believed the serpent rather than God. The consequences of her choice will be felt until the coming of the Lord.

In contrast, Jesus, under the control of the Holy Spirit, based His response to temptation on the Word of God. He didn't allow His physical or emotional needs to dictate His decision. Instead, He turned to what He knew to be truth—the Word of God—and thus claimed victory over the enemy.

When faced with temptation, who will you believe? How will you know whether you are right or wrong? How will you know what choices to make? We have seen from the passages this week the importance of the Word of God in our decision-making process. The psalmist also showed us that it isn't enough to simply "know" what the Word of God says; true victory can only come through meditating on the Word and embracing it.

When confronted with the truth of the Word, we have a choice to make. We can either accept it or reject it. Accepting the Word as truth may mean having to adjust our thought patterns, responses, reactions, and lifestyle to bring them in line with what the Word says.

Many times we are encouraged when we read the Word and see that we are already living it out in our lives. However, should we choose to reject the Word, we will suffer the consequences of our disobedience. You may believe these consequences are temporary, small and seemingly insignificant, affecting only you. But in truth, they have the potential to wreak havoc in your life, in your family's life, and in the world around you, with effects that can last a lifetime.

The choice is yours. What will you do? Where will you turn when faced with temptation? When your emotions are running wild, how will you respond? Being in this study is a step in the right direction!

This week we are going to see that, if we are truly children of God, we are not alone when we have choices to make. Not only did God give us His Word to show us what choices to make, but to ensure our success He also gave us a Helper, One who enables us to make the wise choices. Let's see what role this Helper was meant to play in our decisions.

OBSERVE

Their teacher told them He was going to leave and return to the Father. What were the disciples to do? For the past three and a half years, Jesus taught and instructed the twelve; now their teacher was about to be taken away. How would they know what to do, how to carry on? Listen to Jesus' promise—a promise not only for them but for every person who chooses to believe in Jesus Christ and follow Him.

Leader: Read aloud John 14:26 and 16:13-14.

- *Have the group say aloud and mark each reference to the **Holy Spirit**, including all synonyms and pronouns, with a cloud:*

JOHN 14:26

"But the Helper, the Holy Spirit, whom the Father will send in My name, He will teach you all things, and bring to your remembrance all that I said to you."

JOHN 16:13-14

13 "But when He, the Spirit of truth, comes, He will guide you into all the truth; for He will not speak on His own initiative, but whatever He hears, He will speak; and He will disclose to you what is to come.

¹⁴ "He will glorify Me, for He will take of Mine and will disclose it to you."

INSIGHT

The Greek word translated as "Helper" in John 14:26 is *parakletos,* a person summoned to one's aid. The term refers to an advisor, a legal advocate, a mediator, or intercessor. This Helper will direct the disciples' decisions and counsel them continually.

DISCUSS

• According to John 14:26, who is the Helper to whom Jesus was referring?

• What did you learn about the Helper from these verses? Who is He? Where did He come from? What did He do? What was His role with the disciples?

OBSERVE

One of the many roles of the Holy Spirit is teaching. He instructs from within and recalls to memory the truths that Jesus taught. The Spirit, therefore, impresses the commandments of Jesus on the minds of His followers and thus prompts them to obedience. Isn't it exciting to see that God has not left you on your own? Instead, He has given you a Helper, One who has come to your aid and will direct your decisions and counsel you continually.

What is even more exciting is that we as believers don't have to wait for the Spirit to come to us; He's already here, present in the moment. Let's take a look to see where He is.

Leader: Read aloud John 14:16-17 and 1 Corinthians 3:16 and 6:19.

• *Have the group say aloud and mark* **Holy Spirit,** *including pronouns and synonyms such as* **Helper** *and* **Spirit of truth,** *with a cloud:* ⌒‿⌒

JOHN 14:16-17

16 "I will ask the Father, and He will give you another Helper, that He may be with you forever;

17 that is the Spirit of truth, whom the world cannot receive, because it does not see Him or know Him, but you know Him because He abides with you and will be in you."

1 CORINTHIANS 3:16

Do you not know that you are a temple of God and that the Spirit of God dwells in you?

1 CORINTHIANS 6:19

Or do you not know that your body is a temple of the Holy Spirit who is in you, whom you have from God, and that you are not your own?

DISCUSS

• John 14:16-17 records Jesus speaking to His disciples shortly before His death. What was His promise with respect to the Holy Spirit in these verses?

• In the other two verses, the apostle Paul was writing to Christians living in Corinth. Of what did he remind them with respect to the Holy Spirit?

• Summarize what you learned from these verses in John and 1 Corinthians regarding the believer's relationship to the Holy Spirit.

OBSERVE

Isn't this exciting? God's Spirit will be in you and me forever, guiding and teaching us. We don't have to call and make an appointment; we don't have to wait for His arrival in order to make a decision.

We've seen in the previous passages how God has demonstrated His love for us, helping us to succeed in our walk with Him by the wonderful provision He has made in sending His Holy Spirit. God's Spirit dwells within us forever, guiding us, and teaching us in the ways of truth and righteousness in all that we do. Therefore, we no longer have to make choices on our own.

But what is our responsibility to be in all of this? Let's take a look at the book of Galatians for the answer to that question.

Leader: Read Galatians 5:16-18. Have the group say aloud and mark ...

- *every reference to **the Spirit** with a cloud:* ⟨☁⟩
- *each appearance of **the flesh** with a slash, like this:* ╱

GALATIANS 5:16-18

16 But I say, walk by the Spirit, and you will not carry out the desire of the flesh.

17 For the flesh sets its desire against the Spirit, and the Spirit against the flesh; for these are in opposition to one another, so that you may not do the things that you please.

18 But if you are led by the Spirit, you are not under the Law.

INSIGHT

The word *walk* in this passage means "to behave, conduct yourselves, lead a life." It is in the present tense in the Greek, indicating a continual, habitual action.

DISCUSS

• What did you learn from marking the references to the Spirit?

• According to this passage, who is responsible for our decisions and behavior? Give the reason for your answer.

• If the Holy Spirit is leading you, how will His presence affect the choices you make?

OBSERVE

How can people determine whether or not they are walking by the Spirit? Let's see what we can learn from Galatians 5.

Leader: Read Galatians 5:19-21 aloud. Have the group say and mark...
 • *the flesh* with a slash, as before.
 • *the Spirit* with a cloud.

Leader: Now read the text again and have the group number the deeds of the flesh.

DISCUSS

• The first three deeds of the flesh deal with what kinds of sins?

• Discuss how knowing this will affect the choices you make concerning the things you read, watch, listen to, and wear.

• How will knowing this affect your speech and your relationships?

GALATIANS 5:19-21

19 Now the deeds of the flesh are evident, which are: immorality, impurity, sensuality,

20 idolatry, sorcery, enmities, strife, jealousy, outbursts of anger, disputes, dissensions, factions,

21 envying, drunkenness, carousing, and things like these, of which I forewarn you, just as I have forewarned you, that those who practice such things will not inherit the kingdom of God.

• The next two deeds (numbers 4 and 5) of the flesh deal with religious sins. What are they?

INSIGHT

Idols include not only statues and false gods but anything more important than your walk with God.

• What kinds of things could become idols in your life?

• Based on this passage and your knowledge of God's Word, what decisions should be made concerning psychic hot lines, Ouija boards, horoscopes, and the like? Is "white magic" acceptable? What about Halloween, tarot cards, wicca? If these things involve sorcery, do they have any place in a believer's life? Would the Spirit of God lead you into these things?

• The third group of deeds (numbers 6 through 13) are tied to our interactions with others. Some call these deeds "social offenses." Discuss each one and how it affects the choices we make. For example, road rage and other fairly recent trends indicate anger is a major problem these days. According to this passage, is it acceptable to explode at someone in anger? What if someone's actions provoked your anger?

• Discuss the last two deeds (numbers 14 and 15) of the flesh. What are they and how do they impact the lives of others and the choices we make? Does this list cover every deed of the flesh? Explain your answer from what you see in the text.

INSIGHT

The word translated as *practice* is in the present tense in the Greek. This means *habitual* continuation of fleshly deeds as opposed to *isolated* lapses. It does not mean that a Christian who falls into a single sin loses his salvation. The strong contrast shows that those who continually practice such sins give evidence of never having received God's Spirit.

• According to verse 21, what will happen to those who practice these things?

GALATIANS 5:22-25

22 But the fruit of the Spirit is love, joy, peace, patience, kindness, goodness, faithfulness,

23 gentleness, self-control; against such things there is no law.

24 Now those who belong to Christ Jesus have crucified the flesh with its passions and desires.

25 If we live by the Spirit, let us also walk by the Spirit.

OBSERVE

Leader: Have the group read Galatians 5:22-25 aloud. Once again mark...
  • *the flesh with a slash.*
  • *the Spirit with a cloud.*

DISCUSS

• The word *but* signals a contrast. What is being contrasted in this passage?

• In verse 22 what does the singular verb *is* tell you about the fruit of the Spirit?

• How many aspects of the fruit of the Spirit are there? Say them aloud as a group and number them.

• What is the fruit of the Spirit, and what makes it possible for believers to have this fruit evident in their lives? In answering this question you might want to see every place you marked *the Spirit.*

• How will being aware of the fruit of the Spirit help you to make choices when faced with difficult circumstances? Is it possible to have joy, peace, and patience? How?

• How will knowing these truths help you with choices in regard to your relationships with others? For example, how do you respond to a person who consistently "pushes your buttons"?

• How will knowing that self-control is the fruit of the Spirit affect your choices concerning sexual desires, the way you eat, the time you spend "surfing the net," what you choose to watch and participate in, or the time you spend playing video games?

WRAP IT UP

According to Ephesians 1:13-14, every believer has the Spirit of God dwelling in them. The Holy Spirit is present to direct your decisions and counsel you continually. He teaches and brings to remembrance the things the Lord has said. He dwells within you and glorifies God. You no longer have to make choices on your own; He will guide and direct you—if you will listen. As we have seen, victory comes when you obey the Spirit's leading and the Word of God. Failure is the result of not consistently meditating on the Word and listening to the Holy Spirit. Choices flow out of worldviews and worldviews out of whatever we feed our minds.

Remember that Jesus knew God's Word and clung to it when faced with temptation, and as a result God blessed Him and us. David, however, knew the Word of God yet chose to ignore it and follow his own desires. The consequences were tragic.

You have been given the resources: the Word and the Holy Spirit. The choice is yours. Will you walk according to the Word of God, being led by the Spirit? Or will you choose to disregard the Spirit's leading and follow after your fleshly desires?

If you choose to sin, remember that you can't choose where sin will lead you. A choice for instant gratification of your fleshly desire can bring consequences that last a lifetime; even worse, it can bring death to you or to those you love.

On the other hand, friend, should you choose to walk according to the Word, being led by the Spirit, God will bless you more than you ever imagined possible!

This unique Bible study series from Kay Arthur and the teaching team of Precept Ministries International tackles the issues with which inquiring minds wrestle—in short, easy-to-grasp lessons ideal for small-group settings. The study courses in the series can be followed in any order. Here is one possible sequence:

How Do You Know God's Your Father?

by Kay Arthur, David and BJ Lawson

So many say "I'm a Christian," but how can they really know God's their Father—and that heaven's home? The short book of 1 John was written for that purpose—that you might *know* that you really do have eternal life. This is a powerful, enlightening study that will take you out of the dark and open your understanding to this key biblical truth.

Having a Real Relationship with God

by Kay Arthur

For those who yearn to know God and relate to Him in meaningful ways, Kay Arthur opens the Bible to show the way to salvation. With a straightforward examination of vital Bible passages, this enlightening study focuses on where we stand with God, how our sin keeps us from knowing Him, and how Christ bridged the chasm between humans and their Lord.

Being a Disciple: Counting the Real Cost

by Kay Arthur, Tom and Jane Hart

Jesus calls His followers to be disciples. And discipleship comes with a cost, a commitment. This study takes an inductive look at how the

Bible describes a disciple, sets forth the marks of a follower of Christ, and invites students to accept the challenge and then enjoy the blessings of discipleship.

How Do You Walk the Walk You Talk?

by Kay Arthur

This thorough, inductive study of Ephesians 4 and 5 is designed to help students see for themselves what God says about the lifestyle of a true believer in Jesus Christ. The study will equip them to live in a manner worthy of their calling, with the ultimate goal of developing a daily walk with God marked by maturity, Christlikeness, and peace.

Living a Life of True Worship

by Kay Arthur, Bob and Diane Vereen

Worship is one of Christianity's most misunderstood topics. This study explores what the Bible says about worship—what it is, when it happens, where it takes place. Is it based on your emotions? Is it something that only happens on Sunday in church? Does it impact how you serve? This study offers fresh, biblical answers.

Discovering What the Future Holds

by Kay Arthur, Georg Huber

With all that's transpiring in the world, people cannot help but wonder what the future holds. Will there ever be peace on earth? How long will the world live under the threat of terrorism? Is a one-world ruler on the horizon? This easy-to-use study guide leads readers through the book of Daniel, which sets forth God's blueprints for the future.

Kay Arthur, executive vice president and cofounder of Precept Ministries International, is known around the world as a Bible teacher, author, conference speaker, and host of national radio and television programs.

Kay and her husband, Jack, founded Precept Ministries in 1970 in Chattanooga, Tennessee. Started as a fledgling ministry for teens, Precept today is a worldwide outreach that establishes children, teens, and adults in God's Word, so that they can discover the Bible's truths for themselves. Precept inductive Bible studies are taught in all 50 states. The studies have been translated into 65 languages, reaching 118 countries.

Kay is the author of more than 120 books and inductive Bible study courses, with more than 5 million books in print. She is sought after by groups throughout the world as an inspiring Bible teacher and conference speaker. Kay is also well known globally through her daily and weekly television and radio programs.

Contact Precept Ministries International for more information about inductive Bible studies in your area.

Precept Ministries International
P.O. Box 182218
Chattanooga, TN 37422-7218
800-763-8280
www.precept.org

ABOUT DAVID AND BJ LAWSON

David and BJ Lawson serve as directors of the student ministry of Precept Ministries International. Both have been involved in Precept Ministries since the early 1980s and became staff members in 1997. David, a former police officer and pastor in Atlanta, is a coauthor with Kay Arthur and others of the *International Inductive Study Series* and a teacher on the *Precept Upon Precept* videos. BJ is a speaker and teacher for conferences and seminars. Both serve as trainers, working throughout the United States.